70 Japanese
Gestures

No Language Communication

Hamiru·aqui

Translated by
Aileen Chang

D0834686

Stone Bridge Press
Berkeley, California

Published by
Stone Bridge Press
P.O. Box 8208
Berkeley, CA 94707
TEL 510-524-8732 • sbp@stonebridge.com • www.stonebridge.com

Copyright ©2004 by Hamiru-aqui
Translated by Aileen Chang
Edited by Barbara Bayer

Originally published in Japan in 2004 by IBC Publishing, Tokyo.

Printed in the United States of America.

2010   10 9 8 7 6 5

ISBN 978-1-933330-01-3

Preface

Japanese is considered to be an extremely difficult language to learn. The writing system is made up of over 100 phonetic symbols in addition to thousands of Chinese characters. It is often said that it takes till the age of 10 for a Japanese child to master the language.

Many people are of the belief that Japanese keep body action to a minimum when speaking, yet over 120 gestures are commonly used. Even after eliminating those that will probably no longer be in use by the end of the next decade, 70 still remain. These are presented in this book.

It is an unfortunate fact that, at present, there are many Japanese who are not proficient in English. Communicating with words may be difficult but why not start with gestures? Great insight into the culture and lifestyle of Japan can be had from understanding its gestures.

Many gestures have been influenced by the West and introduced through foreign movies. However, there still are many interesting gestures considered unique to Japan.

This book presents a mix of popular gestures, slang gestures, and gestures used by children. They range from the serious to the downright hilarious.

Also, we recommend that you watch Japanese *manga* and movies in order to better your understanding. In comic strips, animated films, and old films by Kurosawa and Yasujiro Ozu, emotions and meanings not conveyed through words or facial expression are very often expressed with gestures. The reader will be able to recognize many of these after reading this book.

Armed with an understanding of many new expressions, readers will be sure to enjoy a great deal more of the Japanese and the Japanese language.

Hamiru • aqui

CONTENTS

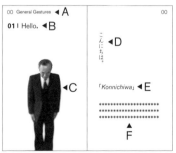

A   Chapter
    Page Number
B   Index Number
    English Gesture Title
C   Gesture Samples
D   Japanese Gesture Title
E   How it is read in Japanese
F   Explanation

General
Gestures

The following are gestures used
in daily life and are popular with
both adults and children.

01 | Bowing

おじぎ

「 *Ojigi* 」

Lower your head.

A movement when greeting someone.

This is a practice that is not seen in Western countries, though it is very often observed in Japan. It is believed to have its roots in China, where it indicates a degree of respect or gratitude to another person. Though Japan does not have the custom of shaking hands, bowing can be looked upon as similar to the Western handshake. It seems that, in general, people bow more politely when bidding goodbye than when meeting someone. When bidding goodbye to an older person or higher-ranked person, to wait with your head bowed until the person turns his/her back, or until the door closes, is a form of showing respect to that person.

02 | Yes. No.

Yes.   No.

はい。
いいえ。

「 *Hai.* 」
「 *Iie.* 」

As in the West, in Japan, one nods when saying "yes" and shakes the head sideways when saying "no."

However, depending on the question, there are times when the English "yes" and "no" seem to be interchanged.

(i.e.) "Aren't you going?"
– "Yes" (nodding the head) = ("Yes, I am not going.")

In the West this question would be answered with a "No" and a shake of the head: "No, I'm not going."

03 | *Itadakimasu.*

Gochisohsama.

ごちそうさま。
いただきます。

「*Itadakimasu.*」
「*Gochisohsama.*」

Place both palms together and lightly bow your head.

Itadakimasu is said before eating a meal.

Make sure your chopsticks are still on the chopstick rest.

Gochisohsama is said after eating a meal.

Both phrases are said while you lightly bow your head.

04 | Me

私

「*Watashi*」

Put your index finger on the tip of your nose.

In Western countries, people point to their chests when indicating themselves, but in Japan, people point to their noses. When indicating others or other things one points with the index finger to the center of the object or the person being indicated. When indicating the person one is talking to directly, the index finger is pointed at his or her nose to indicate "you." The gesture may offend a Westerner, but to the Japanese, it is not considered rude at all. For young people these days, pointing to the nose has become an outdated gesture, and, influenced by movies, they have started pointing to their chests. Nonetheless, pointing to the person one is talking to is still a common Japanese gesture.

05 | Come over here!

Go away!

あっちいけ！
こっちにおいで！

「*Kotchi ni oide!*」

Come over here!
With the back of your hand facing upward, shake your hand downward toward yourself. Some people use both hands to gesture to a child.

「*Atchi ike!*」

Go away!
With the back of the hand facing upward, shake your hand as if trying to shake something off.

Sometimes, the "come over here" gesture may be misunderstood as "go away." The two can be difficult to distinguish, but a nodding of the head, and the fact the person is looking at you and laughing, will make it likely that "come here" is meant. A person saying "go away" will often not make eye contact.

06 | Calm down.

落ち着いて。

「*Ochi tsuite.*」

Move both hands up and down while saying "*maaah maaah maaah*" with your palms facing the ground.

This conveys that one wants a person to calm down, cool his temper, or not be so frantic.

Maaah maaah maaah must be said together with the hand motion. If not, people will not understand what you are trying to say. It may be best to remember the *maaah maaah maaah* and the hand motion as one set.

07 | I'm going to pass in front of you.

前を通ります。

「*Mae wo tohrimasu.*」

Round the back slightly, place one hand up with your fingers together and the thumb up, then gently move your hand up and down when passing in front of someone.

It is basically considered impolite to directly pass in front of someone. This gesture can be taken as an apology when passing in front of someone and obstructing his view, for example, in a store aisle. In Western culture, this gesture is very similar to saying "excuse me" when passing in front of someone.

You will make a positive and favorable impression with this gesture and may find people striking up a conversation with you.

08 | I don't know.
That's wrong.

違う。

知らない。

「*Shiranai.*」
「*Chigau.*」

Shake your upright hand near your mouth with your thumb closer to your face.

There are times when the head is shaken at the same time. In that case, the head and hand will move in opposite directions. When this gesture is seen, for example, when asking directions, it simply means the person does not understand English or he is unable to assist you. One is advised to simply go and ask another person.

09 | Thank you.

かたじけない。

「*Katajikenai.*」

With your thumb facing toward your face, move your hand upright to a point in front of your face.

It is the same gesture made by a *sumo* wrestler who has won as he accepts his prize money.

It is an expression derived from the handheld sword. Often it is used by men as an abbreviated form of expressing appreciation.

In Japan, there is a custom to pour drinks for one's guests. When the host sees his guest's glass is nearly empty, he will come over to refill it. Then, the guest will make this gesture to show appreciation instead of saying "thank you" in words.

10 | Do you want to go eat?

食
事

「*Shokuji*」

Pretend to hold a rice bowl in one hand and bring a chopstick to your mouth with the other hand. Repeat the hand motion of bringing a chopstick to your mouth several times. Sometimes, only the chopstick motion is used with two fingers acting as a chopstick.

When you see someone looking at you and making this gesture, he is asking if you have already eaten or would like to go eat together. Japan is the only country in Asia where spoons are not often used for eating. The Japanese custom is to eat with a rice bowl and chopsticks. Of course when Western dishes are eaten, Japanese will use a fork and spoon. At a formal Japanese dinner, chopsticks only are used. For your additional information, it is not considered impolite to drink soup directly from the bowl. You should also remember to always hold the rice bowl by supporting it with one hand underneath it.

11 | Wait a moment.

ちょっと待って。

「*Chotto matte.*」

Show the palm of one hand to the other person. It also means to wait there. Both hands are used at times.

In the West, gestures meaning "wait" often involve raising your index finger. However, in Japan, showing the palm of one hand or both palms to the other person is the basic gesture. If the Western-style gesture for "wait" is made in Japan, the Japanese would think of it as "1," as in No. 1.

If a child grabs your finger when you point it upward to signify the Western "wait," you will now be aware that it's because he thinks you are starting a game.

Refer to **55** | Grab this finger! on p.122

12 | *Seiza*

Indian-style (*Agura*)

Seiza   Indian-style (*Agura*)

正座　あぐら

「Seiza」

The proper way to sit in a *tatami* room is in the *seiza* position, which is sitting on your knees with your legs tucked under you. In a formal setting, you would continue sitting in the *seiza* position. But once the greetings have been made and the atmosphere becomes relaxed, you may unfold and cross your legs, in the seating position Japanese call "*agura*." The host may sometimes say, "Please put yourself at ease." In which case, you would thank him before assuming the Indian-style position.

「Agura」 Indian-style

Agura was considered a man's seating position from the time when the Japanese dressed mainly in *kimono*. Sitting in the *agura* position was considered bad manners for women. Unless in the company of close friends, it may be better for women to sit with legs unfolded, but to one side. Sitting in the *seiza* position for hours is painful even for many Japanese. The legs fall asleep and you may not be able to stand without help. There are various ways to survive long hours of *seiza* sitting. The most popular one is to cross your toes. Ask a Japanese friend for tips. You will be surprised to find out how many different ways there are.

13 | Tapping the shoulder

肩
を
叩
く

「*Kata wo tataku*」

When you want to let someone know he has dropped something, or you want him to notice that you want to talk to him, or when you're meeting someone and approaching him from behind, tap the person on his shoulder two or three times to make him aware of your presence or to request his attention. The same thing is done when you want to point something out to him, for example, "Look over there!" You would tap the person on his shoulder before saying what you have to say.

Here is a joke that was once popular. You tap a person's shoulder with your index finger pointing toward his cheek; he turns his face toward you. As he does so your finger touches his cheeks. "Ouch!" he says, and you both chuckle over it.

14 | Hot!

熱
い
！

「*Atsui!*」

When you've touched something hot like a pot, grab the earlobe with the thumb and index finger.

This comes from the fact that the earlobe has the lowest body temperature compared to other body parts. Please don't think of this gesture as meaning someone has lost a pair of earrings.

15 | To laugh

笑
う

「*Warau*」

Covering the mouth when laughing.

In the old days in Japan, for a man to show his teeth indicated weakness or that he was joking. To show one's teeth when laughing was considered bad manners. There used to be a custom where married women painted their teeth black (*ohaguro*). To have white teeth forever meant that the woman had missed her chance to marry. Japanese hide their mouths when laughing because of this custom. However, in present-day Japan, there are many who do this in order to hide poor tooth alignment or because they feel embarrassed about something.

16 | Let's put that subject aside.

その話はおいといて。

「*Sono hanashi wa oitoite.*」

The gesture looks like one is moving a box from in front of one's self to the side.

It is a gesture used when changing the subject or saying, "Let's put that subject aside and change the topic."

17 | I agree!

納
得
！

「*Nattoku!*」

Hit the palm of one hand with a closed fist.

This gesture can also be done by hitting your thighs. In that case, be sure to slap your thighs hard enough for the sound to be heard.

This gesture may look similar to a "want to fight" gesture in the West. Don't worry if you see someone directing this gesture at you. There is no need to move away. No one wants to start a fight with you. In fact, it is quite the opposite. They are agreeing with what you say!

18 | Peek

のぞく

「*Nozoku*」

Place your slightly rounded hand against your forehead.

When someone makes the above gesture, he usually means "looking far away." Some people may stretch the bottom of the nose while making the "looking far away" gesture.

When children make a peek gesture, they may make tubes of their fingers and pretend to be looking through binoculars.

19 | Looks delicious!

おいしそう！

「*Oishi soh!*」

Slide the back of one hand along the curve of the chin, or pretend to wipe off some drool.

This is a *manga*-like expression and rarely seen on formal occasions. However, when someone is cooking a special dinner for you, he or she may be happy to see you make this gesture.

20 | *Hidari uchiwa*

左
う
ち
わ

「 *Hidari uchiwa* 」

Fanning (an *uchiwa* is a fan) yourself slowly with your left (*hidari)* hand.

This gesture indicates a comfortable life. It can also mean that you are congratulating yourself, or that you are easy-going and relaxed. Other meanings include "I'm rich," "I don't have to work," and "I'm making a lot of money."

21 | Just hopping mad

おかんむり

「*Okanmuri*」

Point both index fingers above your head like horns, as in the horns of an ogre.

In Japan, this gesture is called *okanmuri*. When a married man says "*okanmuri*" while making this gesture, there is a good chance that he means his wife is angry.

This gesture is only used when referring to someone else.

22 | Ghost

おばけ

「*Obake*」

Hang both hands downward with the backs facing forward.

The gesture resembles something that has had all the life sucked out of it. Do you think the choreographer of "Thriller" got his dance idea from this? Japanese ghosts, however, wouldn't dance or move like "Thriller" dancers.

23 | Pointing a finger

ゆびを指す

「*Yubi wo sasu*」

A Japanese will point his finger at you to indicate "you." Since words such as you, I, and names are often omitted when speaking Japanese, the subject is sometimes made clear by pointing at it. It is not a popular practice in the West, but is by no means considered rude in Japan.

24 | No, that's not the case.

そんなことないです。

「*Sonna koto nai desu.*」

Shake one or both hands with the palm facing the other person.

This gesture is mostly used when denying a compliment.

It means "Oh, not me" or "I don't deserve such a compliment" and expresses modesty or a lack of self-confidence.

25 | This way please.
Please sit here.

こちらへどうぞ。

こちらにお座りください。

「*Kochira e dohzo.*」
「*Kochira ni osuwari kudasai.*」

Show the palm of your hand to the other person and motion with it to the place you wish to indicate.

This is the most polite way to indicate where a person should go or sit. The fingers are together and the tip of the middle finger is directed at the person's feet and the place where he should walk or take a seat. The direction of one's eyes is an important part of this gesture. The person showing the way will look downward in the direction being indicated. This gesture is often seen at temples, shrines, traditional Japanese-style hotels, or at Japanese restaurants.

26 | Line of vision

視
線

「*Shisen*」

In Western culture, one looks directly into the eyes of the other person. This is not the custom in Japan. On the contrary, it is thought impolite to look directly at a person for an extended period of time.

Most people, in fact, would feel uncomfortable being looked at for a long time unless they were in an intimate relationship with that person.

Also, it would probably work against one to keep looking at a woman in hopes of picking her up at a cafe or such.

This is also used in Japan to mean "to look" as when one looks at something so intently that one forgets the time or when one just keeps looking at something for an extended period of time, as in "to look at it enough to bore a hole in it." This expression gives an indication of how strongly Japanese feel about visibility.

Also, when a Japanese person is focused on a conversation, there are times when the eyes are closed in deep thought, not a custom seen in other countries. It does not mean the person has fallen asleep.

Slang
Gestures

Discriminatory gestures

Yes, these do exist in Japan as well. Though it's not advisable to use them too often, they are good for a laugh!

Explanation of slang star
★ ★ ★ ★ ★

For the chapter on Slang Gestures, we have used stars to indicate the strength of the meaning conveyed. The more stars, the more angry a person may become if you direct the gesture at him.

27 | Stupid

くるくるパー

「*Kuru kuru paaah*」

★ ★ ★ ★ ★

Turn a closed fist twice while pointing the index finger at your temple.

Just turning the fist means the same thing but following that by opening the hand facing up increases the degree of stupidity being indicated. It will also increase the anger of the person this gesture is directed at. Opening your hand more strongly and slowly adds to the effect and merits a 10 star rating. If you see someone tapping his temple with the tip of his index finger several times, it means, "Have you gone mad?" This gesture does not mean "to think" as it does in the West. It rates a ★ ★ ★ ☆ ☆ .

28 | To be proud of
To be conceited

てんぐ

鼻が高い

「*Hana ga takai*」

「*Tengu*」

★ ★ ★ ☆ ☆

Make a fist, knuckles up, and place it on the tip on one's nose (for added effect, use both fists, one after the other).

This expression and the gesture means "to be proud of something" and "to have confidence in oneself." When a person is called a *tengu* it means he or she is conceited. The long-nosed *tengu* is a mythological spirit believed to live in the mountains.

29 | Ugly

ブ
ス

「*Busu*」

★ ★ ★ ★ ★

Push up the nostrils with the index finger.

This comes from the notion that an upturned nose is an ugly feature. It is mostly used to convey the appearance of a woman.

In Japan, it is thought embarrassing to show wide-open nostrils to others. The pig in Japan is a symbol of ugly and dirty things. Comedians and actors, when wishing to indicate an ugly person or express that they are playing an ugly person, will sometimes tape the tip of their noses to their foreheads and even color their nostrils black. When you want to make fun of a fat person in Japanese you can say "*buta-yaro*" (you fat jerk) or "*buta*" (pig). This expression warrants a rating of five stars.

30 | Buckteeth

出
っ
歯

「*Deppa*」

★ ★ ☆ ☆ ☆

Cup your hand in front of your mouth with the fingers straight and pointed at a downward angle from your face.

There are many Japanese celebrities who are popular because of their buckteeth and so, in Japan, being buck-toothed may not stop you from enjoying a storybook romance. Not so long ago, a sharp, protruding incisor was considered a cute feature for women. Thus, there were many pop idols in the '80s with vampire-like fangs.

31 | Pregnant

妊
娠

「*Ninshin*」

★ ★ ★ ★ ★ ★

Make a half circle with both hands or one hand in front of your stomach.

This gesture is not recommended to be performed in front of women since it also means you have gotten a girl pregnant. In Japan, pregnant women are treated very nicely, even better than mothers with small children. When you want to sit in a crowded train or wish to receive great hospitality, we highly recommend putting a ball under your shirt.

32 | Big talk

ほ
ら
ば
な
し

「 *Hora banashi* 」

★ ☆ ☆ ☆ ☆

Open and close your hand in front of your mouth, bending your wrist slightly back when your hand is closed, and pushing your hand forward as you open it.

Even when you are in a strange land and feel unusually confident, don't talk too big, like saying you're a millionaire back home, or make other foolish *oh-bora* (a huge *hora banashi*). And if you are a married man, don't make too much *hora* about being single in an attempt to be a hit with the girls!

33 | *Mayu tsuba mono*

まゆつばもの

「Mayu tsuba mono」

★ ★ ★ ☆ ☆

Mayu = eyebrow, *tsuba* = saliva, *mono* = thing

This is a gesture where you lick the tip of your middle finger and run it across your eyebrow.

You would do this when you doubt what you are hearing.

A *mayu tsuba mono* is something that may deceive you and about which you want to be cautious.

The gesture has many possible origins, but the most popular is from traditional folk tales, where a fox or a *tanuki* (raccoon dog) often disguises itself as a human in order to deceive people. Its magic, however, is rendered powerless when saliva gets on its eyebrow. The gesture has a long history, and is said to have been used since the Heian Period (794–1185).

34 | Those people are in the midst of
a fight or argument

喧
嘩
中

「*Kenkachuh*」

★ ☆ ☆ ☆ ☆

Make a cross with the index fingers of both hands, then move one finger in front of the other in rapid succession. This imitates fighting with *katana* (Japanese swords).

You will hardly see any Japanese fighting with *katana* in Japan nowadays.

If by any chance, you see people fighting using *katana*, don't just stand there taking photos! Run away at once!

35 | Gay

おかま

「*Okama*」

★ ★ ☆ ☆ ☆

This gesture means gay if you remain silent.

If you say something, it means that you are whispering about someone behind his or her back.

Gay TV personalities are becoming very popular in Japan among Japanese women. The type of gay men popular in Japan do not have a particular look, but tend to be people who give critical advice on women's fashion.

36 | Japanese Mafia

や
く
ざ

「*Yakuza*」

★ ★ ★ ★ ★

Pretend to draw a line with the nail of your index finger from the ear to the chin.

This indicates a scar gotten from fighting or such.

In general, *yakuza* (Japanese Mafia) value traditions, are well behaved, and respect their elders. Be sure to be on your best behavior when meeting them.

37 | To be arrested

逮
捕

「*Taiho*」

★ ☆ ☆ ☆ ☆ ☆

Lightly make fists of both hands and place both wrists together (as if being handcuffed).

When making this sign to someone who already has a criminal record it warrants a ★ ★ ★ ★ ☆ rating.

38 | Shoplift

万
引
き

「*Manbiki*」

★ ★ ★ ☆ ☆

Crook the upright index finger.

You can move the finger up and down if you like.

Doesn't this gesture remind you of the famous Captain with a Hook?

39 | You want me to punch you?

なぐってやろうか？

「*Nagutte yaroh ka?*」

★ ★ ★ ☆ ☆

Blow on the fist or shake the fist at the opponent.

This is often used as a friendly gesture. Don't worry. The person making the gesture will not really start a fight with you.

40 | *Dogeza*

土
下
座

⌈ *Dogeza* ⌋

☆ ☆ ☆ ☆ ☆

Kneeling before someone. A gesture of deep apology toward someone you have angered or when you are making a very serious request.

Kneel with the upper body bent over the knees, head bowed to the floor in a gesture of deep respect or gravest apology. It is also a sign of humility and subservience. You must do this when begging forgiveness for an irrevocable mistake. Put your forehead to the ground and keep it there until the other person tells you to lift your head. If you are a hip-hop dancer, the position just might prompt you to lift your legs and start spinning around on your head. However, as this will fail to demonstrate remorse, it will likely earn you five stars!

41 | *Hanaji boooo!*

ハナヂ、ぶ〜！

「Hanaji boooo!」

★ ☆ ☆ ☆ ☆

Cover your nostrils with your index and middle fingers, and very quickly, in a forceful movement, like water spurting out from a faucet, bring your fingers down past your chin. Or push them out in front of you as though something is pouring out.

This is a comical gesture expressing blood gushing out of your nose. You would do this jokingly, for example, when you see someone of the opposite sex who is totally your type, someone who would make you so excited that blood rushes to your head and causes your nose to start bleeding.

It is not so much an offensive gesture for the other person. Too bad there aren't more times that call for it.

42 | Butter someone up

ごますり

「*Goma suri*」

★ ☆ ☆ ☆ ☆

Rotate one fist on top of the open palm of the other hand.

Derived from the motion of grinding sesame seeds with a mortar and pestle, it is used to signify singing the praises of another person, usually in anticipation of something in return.

43 | Boyfriend

「*Kareshi*」

★ ☆ ☆ ☆ ☆

Point your thumb upright.

Kareshi means a steady boyfriend.

This gesture is categorized as slang, but would not be considered impolite if used in front of others.

Not recommended for use by women.

44 | Girlfriend

彼
女

「*Kanojo*」

★ ☆ ☆ ☆ ☆

Point your pinkie upright.

Kanojo means a steady girlfriend.

This gesture is categorized as slang, but would not be considered impolite if used in front of others.

Not recommended for use by women.

45 | Sex

セックス

「*Sekkusu*」

★ ★ ★ ★ ★

In America, this gesture is the letter "T" in sign language. In old Japan, it meant "sex." This gesture already existed in the Edo Period (1603–1867) and was quite popular. It was also said to have been used before the Edo Period. However, now in the time of Heisei (1989–), it is considered vulgar and is hardly seen anymore although many Japanese do know and understand the meaning. In some regions, the thumb sticking out between the index and middle finger symbolized a penis. Also, some people use the thumb sticking out between the middle and ring finger to mean "breast."

In any case, these gestures are all rather crude and considered vulgar in most parts of Asia. However, in Brazil, a country right behind Japan (see the globe if you don't believe it), this gesture means "good luck and happiness." So, in Brazil, you can find key holders and many other items made in this shape.

46 | How about a drink?

一
杯
ど
う
？

「*Ippai doh?*」

☆ ☆ ☆ ☆ ☆

Extend your thumb and index finger (like the letter "c") and hold them horizontally, as if you were holding an *ochoko*, a small cup used to drink *sake*.

This gesture is categorized as slang, but is not considered impolite. It is mainly used by men. Men would make this gesture when asking a co-worker for a drink after work. It could also be used when asking women.

47 | Was fired.

首になりました。

「*Kubi ni narimashita.*」

★ ★ ★ ☆ ☆

Extend the back of your hand horizontally and slide it in front of your neck as if you were cutting off your head.

This gesture is used when talking about someone that has been fired. When you make this gesture to a person who has, in fact, been fired, it warrants a ★ ★ ★ ★ ★ rating.

48 | Money
Condom

Money   Condom

コンドーム　お金

「*Okane*」
「*Condohmu*」

★ ★ ☆ ☆ ☆

Make a circle with your thumb and index finger (the Western "OK") and hold it flat, horizontally. This means "money."

If this gesture is made in a drugstore it means a condom. The condom can be expressed with the OK sign; in other words, the hand does not have to be held horizontally.

49 | Bribe

賄
賂

「*Wairo*」

★ ★ ★ ☆ ☆

Imitating hiding money inside the collar of the *kimono*. Nowadays, since the majority of Japanese no longer wear *kimono*, this gesture is seen as pretending to hide money inside one's inner suit pocket. Bribery still exists in Japan even though we no longer wear *kimono*.

If you see someone making this gesture and repeatedly opening and closing one side of the jacket, it means he's making tons. He will usually say "*gappo gappo*" while doing this. *Gappo gappo* expresses the millions of yen sliding into his sleeve.

Slang Review

Aitsu no

busu *de*

deppa *no* **kanojo** *ga*

ninshin *shite*

okanmuri *da.*

That guy's ugly, bucktoothed girlfriend is
pregnant and hopping mad.

Omae no

kubi *ni natta*

kareshi *wa*

goma suri,

okama,

kuru kuru,

paaah!

Your boyfriend, who was fired, is always
buttering people up, is totally gay, and is so stupid!

Children's
Gestures

Expressions used in *manga* (comics) or *manga*-like expressions.

These are cute gestures used by children and are derived from TV or comics.

50 | Pedestrian crossing

横
断
歩
道

「*Ohdan hodoh*」

Crossing the crosswalk with one arm up-stretched.

In order to prevent accidents, schools require children to do this when crossing the street so that they are easily visible to drivers. Some districts even leave yellow flags on either side of crosswalks so children can carry them as they cross the street.

A raised arm does not mean that a pedestrian wants a car to stop in the middle of the road or that he wants to say something to the driver. And even though children may be waving flags, it doesn't mean they're surrendering.

51 | Counting

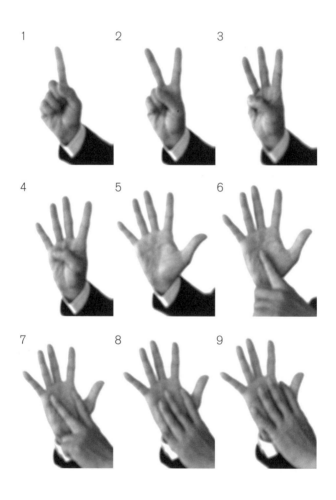

かぞえかた

「*Kazoe kata*」

Use the fingers to express the numbers
one to ten by holding up the corresponding
number of fingers.

10

52 | Finger Family

Thumb - *Oya yubi*
Oya means parent; *yubi* means finger.
That is why a thumb is called *oya yubi*.

Pointing finger - *Hito sashi yubi*
Hito means person; *sashi* means to point;
yubi means finger. Therefore the index
finger is called *hito sashi yubi*.

Middle finger - *Naka yubi*
Naka means center or middle; *yubi*
means finger. Therefore the middle finger
is called *naka yubi*.

Ring finger - *Kusuri yubi*
Kusuri means medicine; *yubi* means
finger. The word *kusuri yubi* comes from
the custom in the olden days of using the
ring finger to mix medicine. The ring finger
was also called *beni sashi yubi* (*beni
sashi* means to apply lipstick) because it
was used to apply lipstick.

Little finger - *Ko yubi*
The word for small or little is *ko*; *yubi*
means finger. Therefore the little finger is
called *ko yubi*.

人指しゆび

親ゆび

ゆび家族

「*Yubi kazoku*」

Children express family members with their fingers.

The thumb is the father finger. The index finger is the mother. The middle finger is the brother. The ring finger is the sister. The little finger is the baby.

53 | Making a vow using your fingers

YU BI   KI RI   GEN MAN   U SO   TSUI TA RA   HA RI SEN BON
ゆ び　き り　げ ん まん　う そ　つ い た ら　は り せん ほん

NO —— MA SU.   YU BI KI —————— TA!!
の —— ま す　ゆ び　き —————— った

ゆ
び
き
り

「*Yubi kiri*」

This gesture is made while singing a song. Children sing while intertwining each other's pinkies of one hand.

The words to the song "*Yubi kiri genman*" mean "if you lie, I will make you swallow 1,000 needles" and are pretty scary. In the Japanese Mafia, breaking a promise or committing some other transgression usually requires that the first knuckle of a finger, usually the pinkie, be cut off.

54 | Please!
Sorry.

ごめん。
お願い！

「*Onegai!*」
「*Gomen.*」

Place both palms together.

This is a gesture used when saying "sorry" or when accepting something while feeling apologetic for having inconvenienced the other person. Although this is a polite gesture, it is usually considered somewhat effeminate. In Japan, the word "*gomen*" is not only an expression of apology but expresses politeness. For instance, in asking a favor, many Japanese would start by saying, "*Gomen* . . ." This could be translated as "I need a favor, but . . . ," "Could you help me?"

When you see Japanese making this gesture, remember, it doesn't mean they're losers, just that they're simply very polite!

55 | Grab this finger!

この
の
ゆ
び
と
ー
ま
れ
！

「*Kono yubi tohmare!*」

When a child wants to start a game with his friends, he will point his index finger up and yell, "*Kono yubi tohmare!*" or "grab this finger!"

Those who want to join in will gather around like bees swarming around a flower, and start grabbing at the finger. If a child grabs your finger when you point it upward to signify the Western "wait!" you will now know that it's because he thinks you are starting a game.

Personally, I would have liked to see someone do this to John Travolta in *Saturday Night Fever* when he made that famous pose. Actually, though, this gesture is usually only made with the finger raised to chest level.

56 | Aren't I cute?

かわいい？

「*Kawaii?*」

Smiling and looking up slightly, touch both index fingers lightly to your cheeks while tilting the head a bit to the side. The gesture can be made with one hand as well.

This is an old expression and was often used by children before the "peace" sign (the "V" sign made with the middle and index finger) became popular.

57 | *Oshiri pen pen!*

おしりぺんぺん！

「*Oshiri pen pen!*」

Oshiri pen pen is the sound of spanking the bottom lightly.

Showing the bottom to another person and patting it is used to ridicule.

58 | Na-nana-na-na.

Sticking out the tongue

舌を出す

あっかんべー。

「*Akkanbaaay.*」

Pull down the lower lid of one eye with the index finger while you say "*akkan*" and stick out the tongue as you say "*baaay.*"

This means "Ugh, I've had it" or "I don't like you." This gesture is equivalent to the taunting "Na-nana-na-na" in America.

「*Shita wo dasu*」

A Japanese girl may stick out her tongue jokingly when she makes a small blunder or slip-up. The gesture can be roughly translated as the English expression "Uh-oh!"

59 | *Jan ken*

じ
ゃ
ん
け
ん

「*Jan ken*」

Commonly done when randomly selecting a person for some purpose, such as deciding the order of players in a game.

Chanting "*jan, ken, pon,*" on "*pon*" the players make one of three shapes with their fists:

Choki = scissors
Pah = paper
Goo = rock

Scissors can cut paper, so scissors win. But scissors can't cut rock, so it loses to rock. And since paper covers a rock, paper wins.

60 | They're deeply in love!

あ
ち
ち
！

「*Achichi!*」

Bend the index fingers of both hands and bring them together several times.

This gesture is often used when a couple is seen being cuddly in public. It's fairly outdated but is still understood.

Achichi can also be roughly translated as "they're hot" in English. This gesture is often used by children to tease young couples. It would not be used toward a husband and wife or toward elderly couples.

61 | Flower

花

「*Hana*」

Spread your fingers wide and place the heels of your palms together in a flower-like ring.

In elementary school, children are often asked to make the flower gesture when receiving a special gift from the teacher, and the gesture is often seen when children sing and dance to songs. If you have the chance to see this gesture, we are certain it will make you smile.

62 | Your underwear is showing

1

「 *Pan* 」

2

「 *Tsuu* 」

3

「 *Maru* 」

4

「 *Mie* 」

ぱんつーまるみえ

「*Pan tsuu maru mie*」

Clap both hands saying "*pan*," raise your index and middle finger in a "V" sign saying "*tsu*" (meaning "two" in English), make a circle with your fingers saying "*maru*" (which means "circle"), bring one palm or both palms to the side of your face as if to peep and say "*mie*" (meaning "to see"). This gesture is mainly used to make fun of someone but it can also be used to warn an unsuspecting person that his underwear is showing without announcing it publicly.

63 | Stars shining brightly

お星さまキラキラ

「*Ohoshisama kira kira*」

Open your fingers and twist your hands at the wrists at or above your head to represent stars sparkling brightly.

Try doing the hand motion while singing "Twinkle Twinkle Little Star." You will be amazed how charming you look!

64 | Peace

ピ
ー
ス

「*Peesu*」

This does not mean "peace" in the literal sense, but is used more for striking a pose for a photograph. This may be considered the equivalent of "hang loose" in the U.S.

This gesture is a common pose for photos.

65 | *Engacho!*

えんがちょ！

「*Engacho!*」

Interlock circles with both index fingers and thumbs and have someone else make a cutting action where your fingers connect.

This is a superstitious gesture that means cutting oneself off from something dirty or unwelcome. Depending on age and region there are said to be two or three different ways of making this gesture. You can see this gesture in the film *Spirited Away* by Hayao Miyazaki.

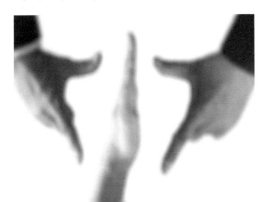

66 | Barrier!

バ
リ
ア
ー
！

「*Bari yaaah!*」

Make a Peace sign (V sign) with each hand and intertwine the middle finger with the index finger.

This represents a barrier you are raising against dirty things or people you don't want to be contaminated by. It means "You can't touch me." There are variations of this gesture depending on age and area. Some say this is *engacho*. However, considering where the gesture comes from, we feel the gesture pictured here is the closest to the original. It may have changed according to how children performed it.

The motion of drawing a triangle using both hands in front of you is also a gesture that expresses a barrier!

67 | Passing by a funeral car

霊柩車が通る

「*Reikyusha ga tohru*」

Hide both thumbs until a funeral car is out of sight.

Because of the saying that one won't be able to see the face of one's parents on their deathbeds, people cover their thumbs, which in Japanese are called *oya* (parent) *yubi* (finger).

This gesture is not used at funerals. It is a superstitious gesture made so one will be able to see the faces of their parents on their deathbeds or wishing that one's parents will not be called by God too soon.

Refer to **52** | Finger Family on p.116

68 | I'm angry

膨れっ面

「*Fukurettsura*」

As a way to communicate their anger, children puff up their cheeks and glower.

The gesture expresses frustration and anger.

This gesture is similar to the facial expression for "fat" in the West. If you see a child making this gesture at you, he in no way means you're fat!

Japanese children will also puff up their cheeks when you say something they don't like or don't want to hear or when they want to complain about something.

Adults use the expression *boo boo iu* (always complaining) when they see children with puffed-up cheeks.

69 | *Banzai!*

万
歳
！

「*Banzai!*」

Throwing both arms up while shouting "*banzai*." Expresses good fortune or happiness.

If the arms are not fully extended but are bent at the elbows, it means surrendering.

After a game, the winning team often does three loud *banzais*, which is collectively called "*banzai sansho*." It is similar to "hip hip hooray" in English. *Doh age* (throwing a person into the air) is also a common practice after a game made up of men only. Players form a circle, throw one of them in the air, catch him as he comes down, then repeat the throw and catch three or four times. In most cases, *doh age* is an act of appreciation to the person being thrown, who is usually the manager or leader of the team or group. If you see this, don't think the people doing this are male cheerleaders!

70 | *Gachohhhhn!*

がちょーーん！

「*Gachohhhhn!*」

Push your hand forward as if throwing a ball and keep your hand open while pulling it back and forth while saying "*Gatchohhhhn!*"

A well-known Japanese comedian made this gesture popular in a TV show. It is mainly used when something is anticlimactic or the outcome is not as anticipated.

Something special for you

Golf

ゴ
ル
フ

This is not a gesture but it is often seen in Japan.

One of the most popular sports for Japanese businessmen is golf.

You will often see people standing on the station platform practicing their golf swing with their umbrellas. If you are a golfer yourself, swinging an umbrella is not taboo by any means. However, doing so in a place where space is limited is dangerous, and therefore earns the five stars. Exclusively for men. One never sees women doing this.

Index

General Gestures

Slang Gestures

Children's Gestures

Model: **Takafumi HAMADA** Engineer

Employed by a major company in Japan until 2002, Hamada was involved in the architectural design of skyscrapers and subway construction and made contributions to society in many areas. He has a deep understanding of Japanese culture and arts.

Design: Morisato TOMURA

iA TOKYO NEWER

Thanks to
Yasuhiro AKITA
Yumi MOTOSHIMA
Toshimune AMIKURA

Hamiru·aqui

A Japanese artist based in Tokyo.

Using black *sumi* (ink) as her main medium, Hamiru is involved in various forms of expression, including art direction, package design, and publishing.

She has written "LE CORBEAU," which was published by the French publisher William Blake & Co. Edit.

She has also written "French Communication through Gestures" and other books.

Hamiru was awarded the 2001 London International Advertising Award.

She hosts the "Tokyo Newer" project team, bringing the new culture of Tokyo to the world.

Aileen Chang

A third-generation Chinese born and raised in Tokyo. Graduated from Sacred Heart University in Tokyo.

Worked at a major advertising agency and is now a freelancer.

Chang is involved in a variety of work from translation and interpretation to planning, making use of the language skills and international sensibility she acquired through her international upbringing.